Fast Kids' Food

Your Promise of Success

Welcome to the world of Confident Cooking, created for you in
our test kitchen, where recipes are double-tested by our team
of home economists to achieve a high standard of success.

MURDOCH BOOKS®

Sydney • London • Vancouver • New York

Fast kids' food

Thbis book is aimed at children aged 6 and up, but don't let the kids have all the fun, the whole family can enjoy these recipes.

Pleasing children is difficult, especially when they seem to prefer everything that is bad for them. Food affects the way children grow, so it is important to give them a balanced diet. This doesn't mean that every meal has to be balanced, just that over each day the foods should add up to a balance. If fruit and vegetables are missing at lunch, make up for it in the afternoon with a snack of vegetable crudites or fruit pieces.

Young children should never be put on a diet, unless you have been advised to do so

by a doctor. All the food groups are essential for growth and development. However, a childhood spent eating junk food is not healthy and will contain far too much fat. Food cooked by you will be far more nutritious and healthy.

Children won't automatically like a new food—don't be disheartened, but try again a few days later. Remember that things that are hated one day can be firm favourites by the following week.

Sweet foods should not be used as rewards or bribes, as this gives them added value in your child's mind.

Children tend to know how much to eat. They eat when they're hungry and until they are full, without having to be forced. Children's appetites also fluctuate, depending on whether they are going through a period of slow or rapid growth. Overweight children tend to be that

way because they are offered too much food. Give small servings and allow for second helpings, so no-one is daunted by the food.

Snacks must be instant and accessible, as well as healthy, otherwise it is easier to open a packet of crisps or biscuits. Try to make fruit always available. Some ideas are nuts, dried fruit, carrot and cucumber sticks, yoghurts, fresh fruit jellies and icy poles made with fruit juice.

Drinks can be high in sugar. Water, fresh juices, fruit milkshakes, whips and cordials are much better than carbonated soft drinks. Add soda water to fruit juices for a healthier fizzy drink and freeze ice-cube trays of orange and lemon juice to add to drinks.

Meat and poultry are often served up to children as fillets and pieces rather than meat on the bone. However, children often like cutlets and chops, chicken drumsticks and wings. Ready-cooked barbecue chickens are useful for sandwiches, tortillas, enchiladas, bakes, pasta dishes and

me-made pizzas.
:babs are fun, but
ke them off the
ewers before giving
very young children.

sh is often seen as
icky to cook, but this
ed not be the case.
hoose very fresh firm-
:shed white fish that
)es not have bones
sk your fishmonger).
sh and chips does not
ive to be a greasy
eal—fish fillets can be
pped in flour then
;htly fried and served
ith baked potato
edges, tomato
:tchup or tartare
uce. Children often
ijoy seafood,
pecially prawns and
lamari rings.

arbohydrates should
rm the biggest part
most meals. Potatoes
e an excellent source
carbohydrates and
n be cooked in many
fferent ways. A
)ring boiled potato
n be transformed into
:licious mash in a
atter of seconds and
ay well be more
:ceptable in this form.
good repertoire of
ash recipes can be
:eful—mix with green
;ggies for bubble and
iueak, with sweet
)tato or pumpkin for
change of colour, or
rve with lots of gravy.

Vegetables are often
the most hated
foodstuff of children
and the hardest to
make sure they eat. If
they prefer vegetables
raw, then don't bother
trying to cook them.
It can be easier to
persuade children to
eat carrot sticks while
watching TV than to
eat cooked vegetables
with their dinner.

Dairy products are
important for children's
calcium intake, as well
as providing a good
source of protein.
Children's calcium
requirements are
high and the
Australian
Nutrition
Foundation
recommends
3 serves of
high calcium
foods (ie dairy
products such
as milk or
cheese) a day.
If you are using
soy milk, make
sure it has
added calcium.

Pulses and grains
can be a great
way of getting
protein into your
child's diet if he
or she is not a
great meat-eater.
They are a good
source of fibre.

The final ingredient for
a healthy child is plenty
of exercise. About
20–30 minutes three or
four times a week is
recommended, but the
more the better.
Exercise is more
enjoyable as a family
affair, and that way
everyone will benefit!

This book is designed
for adults cooking for
children, but most of
the recipes are easy
and many can be
attempted by older
children on their own.
Younger children may
enjoy helping with
the preparation.

3

Fast kids' food

T he serving sizes in this book are reasonably sized and are suitable for adults or older children. Halve if you have younger kids.

Banana apricot muesli muffins

*Ready to eat in
30 minutes
Makes 12 muffins*

1^1/4 cups (155 g) plain
   flour
1^1/4 teaspoons
   bicarbonate of soda
^{3}/4 cup (90 g) untoasted
   muesli
^{1}/2 cup (35 g) All-bran
   cereal
^{3}/4 cup (90 g) sultanas
^{1}/4 cup (45 g) chopped
   dried apricots
^{3}/4 cup (185 g) sugar
^{1}/4 cup (60 ml)
   vegetable oil
^{1}/2 cup (125 ml) milk
1 ripe banana,
   mashed
1 egg
^{3}/4 cup (185 ml)
   buttermilk

Crumble Top
^{1}/2 cup (60 g) plain
   flour
2 tablespoons brown
   sugar
1 teaspoon cinnamon
60 g butter

1. Preheat the oven to moderately hot 200°C (400°F/Gas 6). Sift the flour and bicarbonate of soda into a large bowl, then add all the other dry ingredients. Combine the oil, milk, banana, egg and buttermilk, add to the mixture and fold gently until just combined.
2. For the crumble top, combine the flour, sugar and cinnamon in a bowl. Rub in the butter until it resembles coarse breadcrumbs.
3. Grease or line 12 x ^{1}/2-cup (125 ml) muffin holes and fill to three-quarters full with the mixture. Sprinkle on the crumble top and cook for 20 minutes, or until a skewer inserted into the middle comes out clean. Remove from the tin and cool on a wire rack.

NUTRITION PER MUFFIN
*Protein 2.5 g; Fat 5.5 g;
Carbohydrate 24 g; Dietary
Fibre 1.5 g; Cholesterol
15 mg; 648 kJ (155 cal)*

Banana apricot muesli muffins

Hawaiian french toast

*Ready to eat in
15 minutes
Serves 6–8*

25 g can crushed
  pineapple
eggs
teaspoon vanilla
  essence
tablespoon maple
  syrup
tablespoon caster
  sugar
cup (60 ml) milk
00 g tub plain yoghurt
slices day-old bread
0 g butter

Drain the pineapple
nd place in a food
ocessor or blender
th the eggs, vanilla,
aple syrup, sugar,
lk and a tablespoon
the yoghurt. Process
til smooth, then
ansfer to a shallow
wl or dish.
Trim the crusts from
e bread and halve
ch slice diagonally.
ak a few at a time in
e pineapple batter
til it's well absorbed
both sides but not
o soggy.
Heat half the butter
a large frying pan
til foaming. Fry the
ead in batches over
edium heat until

browned on both sides,
adding the remaining
butter as needed.
Keep each batch warm
as you make the next
batch. Serve warm with
the remaining yoghurt.

NUTRITION PER SERVE (8)
*Protein 15 g; Fat 23 g;
Carbohydrate 47 g; Dietary
Fibre 2.5 g; Cholesterol
230 mg; 1892 kJ (450 cal)*

Note: Honey may be
substituted for maple
syrup if you prefer.

Breakfast apple pancakes

*Ready to eat in
  30 minutes
Serves 4*

30 g butter
1 egg
1 1/4 cups (315 ml) milk
1/4 cup (60 g) caster
  sugar
1/2 teaspoon vanilla
  essence
1 1/2 cups (185 g) self-
  raising flour
2 green apples, peeled,
  cored and grated
butter, for cooking
maple syrup, to serve

1. Melt the butter in a
pan or microwave on
High for 10–15 seconds.
Transfer to a jug and
add the egg, milk, sugar
and vanilla. Whisk

together well.
2. Sift the flour into a
bowl, then gradually
whisk in the liquid
ingredients until you
have a smooth batter.
Stir in the apple. Pour
the mixture back into
the jug for easy pouring.
3. Heat 1 teaspoon of
butter in a large frying
pan until it is foaming,
then add 1/4 cup of the
mixture for each
pancake (depending on
your frying pan, you
should be able to cook
2–3 at a time). Spread
out a little with the
back of a spoon and
cook for 2 minutes, or
until bubbles appear on
the surface. Flip the
pancakes over and
cook for a further
minute on the other
side until golden. Stack
the pancakes on a plate
covered with a tea
towel and keep warm.
4. Cook the remaining
batter, adding more
butter to the pan for
each batch as you need
it. Serve hot with the
maple syrup.

NUTRITION PER PANCAKE
*Protein 3 g; Fat 5 g;
Carbohydrate 20 g; Dietary
Fibre 1 g; Cholesterol
30 mg; 555 kJ (130 cal)*

Note: Different fruit
can be used, such as
dried bananas, fresh
blueberries and
chopped strawberries.

*Hawaiian French toast (top) and
Breakfast apple pancakes*

Chicken stix

*Ready to eat in
  30 minutes
Serves 4–6*

*2 cloves garlic, crushed
2 teaspoons grated
  fresh ginger
1/2 cup (125 ml)
  teriyaki sauce
1 tablespoon honey
1 teaspoon sesame oil
500 g chicken
  tenderloins, halved
  lengthways
3 cups (90 g) cornflakes
3 tablespoons sesame
  seeds*

1. Preheat the oven to moderately hot 200°C (400°F/Gas 6). Combine the garlic, ginger, teriyaki sauce, honey and sesame oil in a large bowl. Add the chicken, toss to coat, then cover and refrigerate until needed.
2. Place the cornflakes in a large plastic bag and crush roughly with your hands (you could get your kids to help out with this). Add the sesame seeds.
3. Drain the chicken, discarding any extra marinade, and place in the bag with the cornflakes. Shake well to make sure the chicken is well coated.
4. Place the chicken on a well-greased baking tray. If any of the coating comes off the chicken, press it back on. Cook for about 10–12 minutes, or until the chicken is cooked through and golden brown. There is no need to turn the pieces over during cooking.
5. Serve hot with a mayonnaise or sweet chilli dipping sauce.

NUTRITION PER SERVE (6)
*Protein 20 g; Fat 5 g;
Carbohydrate 17 g; Dietary
Fibre 1 g; Cholesterol
40 mg; 840 kJ (200 cal)*

Baked ham, egg and cheese rolls

*Ready to eat in
  20 minutes
Serves 4*

*4 round bread rolls
90 g shredded ham
1 1/2 cups (185 g) grated
  Cheddar
4 eggs*

1. Preheat the oven to moderately hot 200°C (400°F/Gas 6). Cut a slice from the top of the rolls and hollow out the bread, leaving a 1 cm wall. Place the bread shells on a baking tray.
2. Divide the ham and 1 cup of the cheese between the rolls, then break a whole egg into the top of each one. Bake for 5 minutes, then remove from the oven and sprinkle with the extra cheese. Return to the oven and bake for 5–7 minutes, depending on how you like your egg cooked.

NUTRITION PER SERVE
*Protein 30 g; Fat 25 g;
Carbohydrate 45 g; Dietary
Fibre 3 g; Cholesterol
230 mg; 2145 kJ (512 cal)*

Note: Process the leftover bread in a food processor and freeze in a plastic bag for breadcrumbs.

*Chicken stix (top) with
Baked ham, egg and cheese rolls*

Mini beef kebabs

*ready to eat in
20 minutes
Makes 12 skewers*

*2 mini bamboo
skewers, about 15 cm
long (see Note)
25 g can pineapple
pieces, drained
zucchini, thickly
sliced into 24 pieces
50 g rump steak, cut
into 2 cm cubes
4 cherry tomatoes
1/4 cup (60 ml)
barbecue sauce*

Place the skewers in
bowl of cold water to
soak. This will stop
them burning while the
kebabs are cooking.
Drain, then thread a
piece of pineapple, a
slice of zucchini, a cube
of steak and a cherry
tomato onto each
skewer. Repeat so that
you have two sets of
ingredients per skewer.
Brush with some of the
barbecue sauce.
Heat a large, non-
stick frying pan and
cook the skewers for
-10 minutes, or
until cooked through,
turning once and
basting with the
remaining barbecue
sauce. Serve with some
steamed rice.

*Mini beef kebabs (top) with
spinach and ricotta frittata*

NUTRITION PER SKEWER
*Protein 5.5 g; Fat 0.5 g;
Carbohydrate 5 g; Dietary
Fibre 1 g; Cholesterol
15 mg; 200 kJ (48 cal)*

Note: If not available,
cut longer skewers
down to size using
kitchen scissors. If you
have more time, soak
the skewers for up to
30 minutes.

Spinach and ricotta frittata

*Ready to eat in
30 minutes
Serves 4*

*250 g orange sweet
potato, cut into
1 cm cubes
2 teaspoons oil
1 clove garlic, crushed
1/2 small red onion,
sliced into thin wedges
150 g English spinach,
trimmed and shredded
60 g ricotta
3 eggs, lightly beaten
1/4 cup (30 g) grated
Cheddar*

1. Place the sweet
potato in a large pan of
salted water and bring
to the boil. Cook for
10 minutes, or until
just tender. Drain well.
2. Meanwhile, heat the
oil in a 20-cm non-stick
frying pan. Add the
garlic and onion and
stir over medium heat
until the onion begins
to soften. Add the
spinach and toss until
the spinach has wilted.
Stir through the cooked
sweet potato and
remove from the heat.
3. Whisk the ricotta
until smooth and
gradually add the eggs
(the mixture may look
slightly lumpy). Season
with salt and freshly
ground black pepper.
Pour the mixture over
the vegetables in the
pan and stir gently,
then swirl the pan to
distribute the egg
mixture evenly. Sprinkle
the cheese over the top.
Preheat the grill.
4. Return the pan to
the heat and cook over
a low-medium heat for
5–8 minutes, or until
the eggs are almost
cooked through. Place
under the grill for
3–5 minutes, or until
the top is set and the
cheese melted. Slide the
frittata out of the pan
and onto a plate,
cheese-side-up, and cut
into wedges. It can be
served hot or cold.

NUTRITION PER SERVE
*Protein 10 g; Fat 10 g;
Carbohydrate 10 g; Dietary
Fibre 2.5 g; Cholesterol
150 mg; 745 kJ (180 cal)*

Note: A wedge of
cold frittata is great
for lunch boxes.

Avocado and tomato salsa with corn chips

*Ready to eat in
15 minutes
Serves 4*

*2 ripe avocados,
 halved
2 ripe tomatoes, finely
 diced
2 spring onions, finely
 chopped
1 Lebanese cucumber,
 finely diced
1 tablespoon olive oil
2 teaspoons white wine
 vinegar
100 g corn chips*

1. Peel the avocados and remove the stone. Dice the flesh and gently toss together in a large bowl with the tomato, spring onion, cucumber, olive oil and white wine vinegar.
2. Serve the salsa piled high in serving bowls, surrounded by the corn chips.

NUTRITION PER SERVE
*Protein 5 g; Fat 35 g;
Carbohydrate 15 g; Dietary
Fibre 5.5 g; Cholesterol
0 mg; 1780 kJ (430 cal)*

Note: You can also use this salsa as a delicious filling for warm soft flour tortillas or lavash bread, or put in a small tub for your child's lunch box.

Chicken kebabs with colourful salsa

*Ready to eat in
20 minutes
Serves 4*

*8 bamboo skewers
4 chicken breast fillets,
 cut into bite-size
 cubes
1/2 cup (125 ml)
 barbecue marinade
1 loaf Turkish bread,
 halved lengthways
 through the centre
lettuce leaves, to serve*

Colourful Salsa
*2 large tomatoes ,finely
 chopped
1 Lebanese cucumber,
 finely chopped
1 peach or nectarine,
 stoned and finely
 chopped
1/2 cup (25 g) chopped
 fresh coriander or
 parsley*

1. Place the skewers in a bowl of cold water to soak. This will stop them burning while the kebabs are cooking. Preheat a grill or barbecue hot plate.
2. Thread the chicken cubes onto the skewers and place in a shallow dish. Coat with the barbecue marinade, cover and refrigerate until ready to use.
3. To make the colourful salsa, combine the tomato, cucumber, peach and coriander in a bowl.
4. Cut the Turkish bread into 8 slices, then grill the cut surfaces.
5. Remove the skewers from the marinade (reserving the marinade) and place in a single layer, well spaced out, on the hot grill or barbecue hot plate. Cook for 3 minutes, then turn and cook for a further 3 minutes until cooked through. Brush with the reserved marinade during cooking.
6. Remove the skewers and arrange the chicken and lettuce leaves on the Turkish bread. Serve with the salsa.

NUTRITION PER SERVE
*Protein 30 g; Fat 3 g;
Carbohydrate 30 g; Dietary
Fibre 3 g; Cholesterol
55 mg; 1130 kJ (270 cal)*

Note: You could use mango or paw paw instead of the peach. Sprinkle the salsa with balsamic vinegar or lemon juice for a more tangy taste. Left-overs will make a delicious sandwich the next day

*Avocado and tomato salsa with corn chips (top)
and Chicken kebabs with colourful salsa*

Chicken burgers

*Ready to eat in
20 minutes
Serves 4*

*50 g chicken mince
spring onions, finely
chopped
1/4 cup (75 g) dried
breadcrumbs
egg
tablespoon oil
rolls
tablespoons
cranberry sauce
1/2 cup (30 g) alfalfa
sprouts*

1. Using your hands,
combine the chicken
mince, spring onions,
breadcrumbs and egg in
a large bowl. Shape
into 8 hamburger
patties, no thicker
than 1.5 cm.
2. Heat the oil in a
non-stick frying pan.
Alternatively, use a
chargrill pan, grill or
barbecue and lightly
brush the burgers with
the oil before cooking.)
Cook the burgers
over medium heat for
4–5 minutes each side,
or until they are
cooked through.
3. Split the rolls in
half lengthways and
top each base with
a chicken burgers,
teaspoons of the
cranberry sauce and
some alfalfa sprouts.
Replace the top of
the roll.

NUTRITION PER SERVE
*Protein 8 g; Fat 15 g;
Carbohydrate 18 g; Dietary
Fibre 1.5 g; Cholesterol
45 mg; 1345 kJ (305 cal)*

Note: Alternative
burger toppings
include mayonnaise
and shredded lettuce,
or just tomato sauce.

Tuna and bean tacos

*Ready to eat in
15 minutes
Serves 6*

*12 taco shells
2 x 185 g cans tuna,
drained
1/2 cup (125 g) sour
cream
1/2 small red onion,
finely chopped
300 g can cannellini
or butter beans,
rinsed and drained
2 cups (90 g) shredded
lettuce
3 tomatoes, finely
sliced*

1. Preheat the oven to
moderate 180°C
(350°F/Gas 4) and
warm the taco shells
for 5–10 minutes while
preparing the filling.
2. Break the tuna into
chunks and combine
with the sour cream,
red onion and the
beans. Season with salt
and freshly ground
black pepper.
3. Place some of the
lettuce and a couple of
slices of tomato in each
taco, then fill with the
tuna and bean mixture.
Serve immediately,
allowing two tacos
per person.

NUTRITION PER SERVE
*Protein 20 g; Fat 15 g;
Carbohydrate 8 g; Dietary
Fibre 4.5 g; Cholesterol
60 mg; 1306 kJ (297 cal)*

Note: The filling for the
tacos also makes a
good lunch box salad.
Put it in an airtight
container and serve
the tacos or corn chips
on the side.

*Chicken burgers (top) with
tuna and bean tacos*

LUNCH BOXES

It is important that children have a healthy and nutritious lunch every day that they actually enjoy eating. A balanced lunch should include carbohydrates such as bread, pasta, rice and potatoes; proteins such as meat, fish, cheese and eggs; and fresh fruit and vegetables. Drinks can be yoghurt or milk drinks, fruit juices or water. Junk food and fizzy drinks won't add much nutritious value to a lunch box and are best left out.

Sandwiches can be made from any type of sliced bread, roll, English muffin or rollable bread such as Lebanese breads or pitta pockets. There are lots of delicious sandwich fillings, but avoid things that will make the bread go soggy or are bland and boring. Including relatively wet fillings such as mashed avocado or banana, hummus, cottage cheese, ricotta or chutneys and pickles means that you don't need to use butter or margarine. Rolled breads can be wrapped

in foil to keep their shape, and sandwiches can be wrapped in baking paper or sealed in snaplock bags. An airtight lunch box will keep everything fresh.

Baked foods such as quiches, frittatas and tartlets are good for lunch boxes, as are savoury muffins and scones. Wrap everything separately in foil or plastic wrap to prevent it becoming soggy. Sweet muffins, giant cookies, health bars and slices are good treats and are better than chocolate bars. Salads packed in separate boxes and served with bread mak

change from
ndwiches. Try
egetable sticks, fruit
ieces or dried fruit
rved with a dip of
ummus or cottage
heese. Or maybe a
asta, rice or potato
lad with chicken,
una or meat. Other
lads that work well in
lunch box include
bbouleh, coleslaw
nd mixed-bean salad.

Drinks in tetrapaks
ich as fruit juices,
oghurt and milk
rinks can be frozen
nd then put straight in
le lunch box. This
leans they will still be
old when lunchtime
omes around and will
elp keep everything
se cool as well.

You can also make
your own fruit juices,
smoothies and shakes,
but make sure you
leave enough room for
the liquid to expand if
you are freezing drinks
in your own containers.

It is important that
lunch boxes are kept
clean and free from
bacteria. Empty out
any uneaten food and
wash the box out daily,
then dry it thoroughly
before storing, leaving
the lid off. If it's a hot
day and your child does
not have a fridge
available for storage at
school, add a frozen
drink or ice pack to
make sure everything
stays chilled until
lunchtime. Choose a
box that is manageable
for your child but has

enough room to hold
everything. Make sure
it has a tight seal
around its lid, but if
your child is very
young, check they can
remove the lid without
any trouble. This also
applies to any packing
materials inside—little
fingers find foil and
snaplock bags much
easier to handle than
plastic wrap.

*Lunchbox recipes from
left to right: a Banana
apricot muesli muffin
(page 4); Spinach and
ricotta frittata (page
11); an Iced banana
smoothie (page 62);
Tuna and bean tacos
(page 21); Fruche and
fruit salad (page 58);
Gado Gado (page 30);
and a Strawberry soy
thickshake (page 62)*

Rice with beef strips

*Ready to eat in
  30 minutes
Serves 4*

1 tablespoon oil
1 small onion, chopped
100 g mushrooms,
  chopped
1 clove garlic, crushed
1 cup (200 g) long-
  grain white rice
1¹/2 cups (375 ml)
  chicken stock
400 g rump steak,
  finely sliced
1 tomato, diced
2 tablespoons chopped
  fresh parsley

1. Heat the oil in a pan,
add the onion,
mushrooms and garlic
and cook over medium
heat for 2–3 minutes,
or until the onion has
softened. Stir through
the rice, then pour over
the chicken stock and
stir to combine. Bring
to the boil, then reduce
the heat to low and
simmer, covered, for
10 minutes. Leaving
the pan covered,
remove it from the heat
and allow to stand for
5 minutes.
2. Meanwhile, heat a
wok or heavy-based
frying pan and cook the
slices of rump steak on
both sides until cooked
through. Cut into thin
strips. Cover, set aside
and keep warm.
3. Add the tomato and
parsley to the rice and
stir the beef strips
through. Season well
before serving.

NUTRITION PER SERVE
*Protein 30 g; Fat 8 g;
Carbohydrate 40 g; Dietary
Fibre 3 g; Cholesterol
65 mg; 1495 kJ (355 cal)*

Pork with rice stick noodles

*Ready to eat in
  30 minutes
Serves 4*

150 g thin rice stick
  noodles
2 tablespoons oil
200 g pork eye fillet,
  thinly sliced
3 cloves garlic,
  crushed
1 carrot, cut into
  matchsticks
50 g snow peas, cut
  lengthways into
  matchsticks
1 tablespoon soy sauce
1 tablespoon lime juice
2 teaspoons soft brown
  sugar
1 teaspoon fish sauce
1 tablespoon chopped
  fresh chives
1 tablespoon chopped
  fresh mint

1. Soak the rice sticks
in boiling water for
5–10 minutes, or until
they are soft. Drain and
set aside on a clean tea
towel to dry.
2. Meanwhile, heat
1 tablespoon of the oil
in a wok or heavy-
based frying pan. When
the oil is hot, fry the
pork slices and garlic,
in batches, until the
pork is cooked through
and browned. (Add
more oil if necessary.)
Remove, set aside and
keep warm.
3. Heat the remaining
oil in the wok or frying
pan and stir-fry the
carrot and snow peas
for 2–3 minutes over a
high heat. Return the
pork slices to the
wok along with the
noodles and toss
everything together.
4. Add the soy sauce,
lime juice, brown
sugar and fish sauce.
Toss together until
well combined.
5. Just before serving,
add the chopped chives
and mint and mix
together well.

NUTRITION PER SERVE
*Protein 15 g; Fat 10 g;
Carbohydrate 15 g; Dietary
Fibre 2 g; Cholesterol
30 mg; 935 kJ (225 cal)*

Note: You can also
use fresh rice noodles
or rice vermicelli for
this dish.

*Rice with beef strips (top) and
Pork with rice stick noodles*

Nachos

*Ready to eat in
30 minutes
Serves 4*

*teaspoons oil
50 g beef mince
00 g can red kidney
beans
00 g jar taco sauce
30 g packet corn chips
cup (125 g) grated
Cheddar
tomatoes, chopped
spring onions, finely
sliced
/2 avocado
tablespoon lemon
juice*

. Preheat the oven to
moderate 180°C
350°F/Gas 4). Heat the
oil in a frying pan and
add the mince. Cook
or 5 minutes, or until
the beef has browned
and most of the liquid
has evaporated,
breaking up any lumps
with a fork. Add the
beans and taco sauce
and cook, stirring, for
another 10 minutes.
2. Divide the mince
mixture between four
ovenproof plates or
shallow soup bowls,
keeping the mixture in
the centre. Arrange the
corn chips around the
edge, tucking them
lightly into the beef
mixture. Sprinkle the
cheese over the beef
and a little way onto
the corn chips. Bake for
5 minutes, or until the
cheese melts.
3. Combine the tomato
and spring onion and
place in the centre of
the nachos. Mash the
avocado with the
lemon juice and place
a spoonful on top of
each dish.

NUTRITION PER SERVE
*Protein 30 g; Fat 27 g;
Carbohydrate 25 g; Dietary
Fibre 10 g; Cholesterol
70 mg; 1954 kJ (467 cal)*

Caramelized chicken wings

*Ready to eat in
30 minutes
Serves 4*

*1 kg chicken wings
2 teaspoons peanut oil
2 cloves garlic,
crushed
1 teaspoon finely
grated fresh ginger
1/4 cup (90 g) honey
2 tablespoons soy
sauce*

1. Cut the tip off each
chicken wing and
discard. Cut the wings
in half at the joint.
2. Heat the oil in a
wok or large heavy-
based frying pan. Add
the garlic and ginger
and cook, stirring, over
medium-high heat for
1 minute. Add the
chicken and stir-fry for
2 minutes until brown.
3. Stir in the honey and
soy and cook, covered,
over medium heat for
10 minutes. Remove
the lid and cook,
stirring occasionally,
for a further 10
minutes, or until the
chicken is tender and
caramelized. Serve as a
snack or with some
steamed rice.

NUTRITION PER SERVE
*Protein 1 g; Fat 12 g;
Carbohydrate 20 g; Dietary
Fibre 0 g; Cholesterol
0 mg; 990 kJ (225 cal)*

*Nachos (top) with
Caramelized chicken wings*

San choy bau

*Ready to eat in
  30 minutes*
Serves 4

*8 small iceberg lettuce
  leaves*
1 tablespoon oil
2 cloves garlic, crushed
*1 stem lemon grass,
  white part only, finely
  chopped*
500 g lean pork mince
1 carrot, finely chopped
*2 spring onions, finely
  chopped*
*60 g water chestnuts,
  finely chopped*
1 tablespoon lime juice
1 tablespoon soy sauce
*2 teaspoons soft brown
  sugar*
*2 tablespoons chopped
  fresh coriander*
Hoisin sauce, to serve

1. Rinse the lettuce
leaves and gently pat
dry. Set aside on a
serving plate.
2. Heat the oil in a wok
or frying pan. Add the
garlic, lemon grass and
pork mince. Stir-fry
over a high heat for
5 minutes, or until the
mince has browned
and cooked through,
breaking up any lumps
with a fork.
3. Add the carrot,
spring onions and
water chestnuts and
toss until well
combined and heated
through. Add the lime
juice, soy sauce, brown
sugar and coriander
and stir in. Spoon
into the lettuce leaves
and serve with some
Hoisin sauce.

NUTRITION PER SERVE
*Protein 30 g; Fat 7.5 g;
Carbohydrate 6 g; Dietary
Fibre 2 g; Cholesterol
60 mg; 885 kJ (210 cal)*

Note: Chicken mince
can be substituted
for the pork mince.

Baked sesame
chicken on toast

*Ready to eat in
  30 minutes*
Serves 4

250 g chicken mince
1 clove garlic, crushed
*1 teaspoon grated fresh
  ginger*
*1 tablespoon oyster
  sauce*
2 teaspoons soy sauce
1 teaspoon sesame oil
*1 tablespoon chopped
  fresh coriander*
1 tablespoon cornflour
*8 slices bread, crusts
  removed*
*1/4 cup (40 g) sesame
  seeds*
*sweet chilli sauce or soy
  sauce, to serve*

1. Preheat the oven to
moderately hot 200°C
(400°F/Gas 6). Mix
together the chicken
mince, garlic, ginger,
oyster and soy sauce,
oil, coriander and
cornflour in a bowl.
2. Spread about
2 heaped teaspoons of
the mixture evenly ont
each piece of bread,
right up to the edges.
3. Spread the sesame
seeds out on a plate.
Dip each piece of
bread, mixture-side-
down, into the sesame
seeds. Place on a
baking tray and bake
for 15–20 minutes, or
until the mixture is
golden and cooked
through.
4. Slice each piece in
half and serve with the
sweet chilli sauce or
soy sauce.

NUTRITION PER SERVE
*Protein 20 g; Fat 10 g;
Carbohydrate 30 g; Dietar_
Fibre 2.5 g; Cholesterol
30 mg; 1220 kJ (290 cal)*

Note: You can make
these sesame toasts
ahead of time and
freeze them before
baking. Layer in a
container with freezer
wrap between each
layer and freeze for up
to 2 months. When
you want to eat them,
defrost, then bake
as above.

*San choy bau (top) wit
Baked sesame chicken on toa*

Noodle pancakes with satay chicken

Ready to eat in
25 minutes
Serves 4

packet of 2-minute
chicken noodles with
the flavour sachet
tablespoons chopped
fresh chives
1/2 cup (125 ml) oil
onion, sliced
50 g chicken
tenderloins or thigh
fillets, sliced into
bite-size pieces
3/4 cup (185 ml) bottled
satay sauce
tablespoon chopped
peanuts
teaspoons chopped
fresh coriander

1. Pour boiling water
over the noodles, allow
them to soften, then
drain well.
2. Place the noodles in
bowl with the flavour
sachet and chives.
Mix well and divide
into four batches.
3. Heat the oil in a
frying pan and fry each
batch, flattening the
noodles out to form a
pancake shape. Turn
the pancake over and
repeat on the other
side. Fry until they are
golden and crispy, then
drain and keep warm.

4. Strain off any
remaining oil in the
pan, leaving just
1 tablespoon. Fry the
onion for 2 minutes,
then add the chicken
pieces and fry until
browned. Add the satay
sauce and peanuts to
the pan and simmer,
stirring, for 5–10
minutes, or until the
chicken is cooked.
5. To serve, place the
noodle pancake on a
plate, spoon the
chicken satay over the
top and sprinkle with
the coriander.

NUTRITION PER SERVE
Protein 18 g; Fat 45 g;
Carbohydrate 15 g; Dietary
Fibre 2 g; Cholesterol
50 mg; 2405 kJ (445 cal)

Mexican burgers

Ready to eat in
30 minutes
Serves 4

1 small onion
450 g beef mince
1/2 cup (40 g) fresh
breadcrumbs
1/4 cup (60 ml) milk
1 tablespoon taco
seasoning mix
2 tablespoons finely
chopped fresh
coriander or
flat-leaf parsley
plain flour, for coating
1 tablespoon butter
2 tablespoons vegetable
oil
4 hamburger buns
4 lettuce leaves, torn
into pieces
200 g jar taco salsa

1. Finely grate the
onion and put in a
large bowl with the
beef mince,
breadcrumbs, milk,
taco seasoning mix and
the coriander or
parsley. Season with
salt and freshly ground
black pepper and mix
well to combine.
2. Divide the mixture
into four and form each
portion into a round
and flattened burger
shape. Lightly coat
with the flour.
3. Heat the butter and
oil in a large frying pan
and add the burgers.
Cook over medium
heat for 8 minutes
each side, or until
cooked through.
4. Slice the buns and
place the lettuce on the
bases. When the
burgers are cooked,
place them on top of
the lettuce and spoon
some taco salsa over
the top. Top with the
other half of the bun
and serve with corn
on the cob.

NUTRITION PER SERVE
Protein 35 g; Fat 30 g;
Carbohydrate 60 g; Dietary
Fibre 5 g; Cholesterol
85 mg; 2670 kJ (640 cal)

Noodle pancakes with satay chicken (top) and
Mexican burgers

Tuna and potato patties

*Ready to eat in
30 minutes
Makes 8*

600 g potatoes, peeled
  and cubed
3 spring onions, finely
  chopped
130 g can corn kernels,
  drained
185 g can tuna, drained
  and mashed
2 tablespoons
  mayonnaise
1 egg, lightly beaten
dry breadcrumbs, for
  coating
vegetable oil, for frying

1. Bring a large pan of salted water to the boil and cook the potatoes for 8 minutes, or until tender. Drain well and mash, then leave to cool a little.
2. Put the mashed potato, spring onions, corn kernels, tuna and mayonnaise in a large bowl and mix together well. Divide the mixture into eight balls and flatten into thick patties.
3. Place the egg in a shallow dish and the breadcrumbs on a plate. Dip each patty into the egg, then coat with the breadcrumbs, shaking off the excess.
4. Put 1 cm oil in a large frying pan. Heat the oil over medium heat until a cube of bread browns in 15 seconds. Add the patties, in batches if necessary, and cook for 3 minutes, then turn and cook for a further 3 minutes, or until golden and cooked through. Drain the patties thoroughly on paper towels and serve with some green vegetables.

NUTRITION PER PATTY
*Protein 10 g; Fat 10 g;
Carbohydrate 20 g; Dietary
Fibre 2 g; Cholesterol
35 mg; 860 kJ (205 cal)*

Zucchini frittata

*Ready to eat in
25 minutes
Serves 4–6*

2 zucchini
1 carrot, finely grated
1 onion, finely chopped
3 bacon rashers, diced
2 teaspoons mixed
  dried herbs
6 eggs
1/2 cup (125 ml) milk
1/2 cup (125 ml) cream
1 tablespoon oil
1/2 cup (60 g) grated
  Cheddar

1. Grate the zucchini into a colander and use your hands to squeeze out any excess liquid. Add the zucchini to the carrot, onion, bacon and dried herbs and combine well.
2. Mix together the eggs, milk, cream and some salt and freshly ground black pepper. Pour into the grated vegetables and combine well.
3. Place the oil in an ovenproof non-stick frying pan, about 28–30 cm in diameter, and heat the oil over medium heat. When hot, add the mixture, turn down the heat to very low and cook for about 10–15 minutes, or until the mixture is almost set in the centre and the sides and bottom of the frittata have a nice golden crust. Preheat the grill.
4. Place the frittata under the hot grill for 3 minutes, then sprinkle over the Cheddar and grill until melted and golden.
5. Slide the frittata out onto a serving plate and slice into wedges. Serve with a green salad or some steamed vegetables.

NUTRITION PER SERVE (6)
*Protein 15 g; Fat 20 g;
Carbohydrate 4.5 g; Dietary
Fibre 1.5 g; Cholesterol
230 mg; 1140 kJ (275 cal)*

*Tuna and potato patties (top)
with Zucchini frittata*

Veal schnitzel with ham, tomato and cheese

Ready to eat in 15 minutes
Serves 4

0 g butter
pieces crumbed veal
schnitzel
slices ham
tomatoes, sliced
cup (125 g) grated
Cheddar

. Preheat the grill to medium-hot.
. Melt half the butter in a large frying pan and fry two of the schnitzels for about –4 minutes on each de. Transfer to a aking tray and osition under the grill ust so they stay warm. ry the last two chnitzels in the remaining butter, then ut them on the tray with the others.
. Top each schnitzel with a slice of ham. arrange the tomato ices in a single layer ver the ham, dividing em among the chnitzels, then season with freshly ground lack pepper. Sprinkle he Cheddar over the op of the tomato.

4. Turn the grill to high and place the plate directly under the heat. Grill until the cheese melts and turns golden. Serve with some steamed vegetables

NUTRITION PER SERVE
Protein 30 g; Fat 40 g; Carbohydrate 1.5 g; Dietary Fibre 1 g; Cholesterol 115 mg; 1369 kJ (310 cal)

Salami and tomato pasta

Ready to eat in 20 minutes
Serves 4

325 g penne pasta
1¹/₂ cups (375 g)
    tomato pasta sauce
4 Roma tomatoes,
    roughly chopped
1 large cabanossi stick
    (about 180 g), sliced
¹/₂ cup (30 g) chopped
    fresh parsley

1. Bring a large pan of salted water to the boil. Cook the pasta according to the manufacturer's instructions. Drain and divide among four serving bowls.
2. Meanwhile, place the pasta sauce and 1 cup (250 ml) of water in a pan. Bring to the boil and cook for 5 minutes, or until the mixture is slightly thickened. Stir

in the tomatoes and cook for a further 2 minutes just to warm the tomatoes through. Add the cabanossi and parsley and heat through. Pour over the pasta, dividing the mixture among the bowls, and serve hot.

NUTRITION PER SERVE
Protein 20 g; Fat 20 g; Carbohydrate 70 g; Dietary Fibre 7 g; Cholesterol 50 mg; 2210 kJ (530 cal)

Note: You can use any variety of mild salami instead of the cabanossi. Different types of pasta shapes can be used in this recipe for variety, or try using one of the coloured pastas for a change.

Veal schnitzel with ham, tomato and cheese (top) with Salami and tomato pasta

29

Gado Gado

*Ready to eat in
  30 minutes
Serves 4–6*

Peanut sauce
*1 tablespoon oil
1 onion, finely chopped
1 clove garlic
1/2 cup (125 g) crunchy
  peanut butter
2 teaspoons soy sauce
140 ml can coconut
  milk
1 tablespoon chopped
  fresh coriander*

Accompaniments
*baked potato wedges
1 celery stick, cut into
  batons
1 carrot, cut into
  batons
4 button mushrooms,
  sliced
4 cherry tomatoes,
  halved
150 g cauliflower
  florets, lightly
  steamed or
  microwaved until
  just tender
150 g broccoli florets,
  lightly steamed or
  microwaved until
  just tender
or your own choice of
  vegetables, raw or
  cooked*

1. To make the peanut
sauce, place the oil,
onion, garlic, peanut
butter, soy sauce and
coconut milk in a
blender with 1/2 cup

(125 ml) water and
blend until mixed. Pour
into a pan and bring
to the boil. Reduce the
heat and simmer for
5 minutes, then add the
coriander. Place the
sauce in a bowl.
2. Place the vegetables
on a large platter with
the sauce in the centre
for dipping. Your kids
can dip the vegetables
straight into the sauce.

NUTRITION PER SERVE (6)
*Protein 9 g; Fat 20 g;
Carbohydrate 8.5 g; Dietary
Fibre 5.5 g; Cholesterol
0 mg; 990 kJ (235 cal)*

Couscous with honeyed chicken

*Ready to eat in
  30 minutes
Serves 4*

*1 1/3 cups (245 g)
  couscous
40 g butter
1/2 cup (75 g) frozen
  corn kernels
1/2 cup (80 g) frozen
  peas
50 g oil or butter
500 g chicken
  tenderloins, trimmed
  and cut into bite-size
  strips
1 tablespoon honey
1 tablespoon lemon
  juice
2 tablespoons chopped
  fresh parsley, optional*

1. Place the couscous
a bowl and pour in
1 1/3 cups (350 ml)
boiling water. Add
the butter. Leave for
4 minutes while you
cook the corn and pea
2. Bring a small pan
of salted water to the
boil and add the corn
and peas. Cook for
2 minutes, then
drain well.
3. Fork the couscous
until light and fluffy
and fold through the
corn and peas. Keep
warm while you cook
the chicken.
4. Heat the oil or butt
in a heavy-based fryin
pan or wok and, whe
it begins to foam, add
the chicken in batches
Cook for 5 minutes,
stirring, until the
chicken is golden and
cooked through. Stir
through the honey and
lemon juice and scrap
up any brown bits in
the pan. Add a little
water if the mixture
appears too dry.
5. Divide the couscous
among 4 serving plate
pile the honeyed
chicken on top and
scatter with the parsle

NUTRITION PER SERVE
*Protein 35 g; Fat 40 g;
Carbohydrate 15 g; Dietar
Fibre 3 g; Cholesterol
55 mg; 2210 kJ (502 cal)*

*Gado Gado (top) an
Couscous with honeyed chick*

Hokkien noodle and beef stir-fry

Ready to eat in
20 minutes
Serves 4

2 tablespoons oil
400 g beef strips
2 cloves garlic, crushed
1 teaspoon grated
fresh ginger
400 g frozen Thai-style
stir-fry mixed
vegetables, thawed
1/3 cup (80 ml) Hoisin
sauce
450 g Hokkien
noodles, separated

1. Heat a wok or
heavy-based frying pan
until very hot, add
1 tablespoon of the oil
and swirl it around to
coat the side of the pan.
Add the beef strips and
stir-fry for 2–3 minutes,
or until just browned
and cooked through.
Remove and set aside.
2. Heat another
tablespoon of oil in the
wok and add the garlic
and ginger. Stir-fry for
10 seconds, then add
the Thai-style vegetables
and stir-fry for 2–3
minutes, or until the
vegetables are tender.
Return the meat to the
wok, add the Hoisin
sauce and Hokkien
noodles and toss well
to combine. Cook for a
further 5 minutes, then
serve immediately.

NUTRITION PER SERVE
Protein 20 g; Fat 15 g;
Carbohydrate 55 g; Dietary
Fibre 8.5 g; Cholesterol
45 mg; 1800 kJ (430 cal)

Sweet and sour chicken stir-fry

Ready to eat in
30 minutes
Serves 4

2 tablespoons oil
300 g chicken breast
fillet, cut into small
cubes
1 small onion, chopped
1 red capsicum, cut
into cubes
2 small carrots, sliced
100 g snow peas, halved
225 g can pineapple
pieces, drained
1/2 cup (125 g) bottled
sweet and sour sauce

1. Heat a wok or
heavy-based frying pan
until very hot, then add
half the oil and swirl it
around to coat the side
of the pan. Add the
chicken in batches and
stir-fry until golden
brown and cooked
through. Remove and
set aside.
2. Heat another
tablespoon of the oil in
the wok, add the onion,
capsicum, carrot, snow
peas and pineapple and
stir-fry for 2 minutes,
or until the onion has
softened slightly.
3. Return the chicken
to the wok, add the
sweet and sour sauce
and toss to coat well
and heat through. Serve
with steamed rice.

NUTRITION PER SERVE
Protein 20 g; Fat 10 g;
Carbohydrate 25 g; Dietary
Fibre 3.5 g; Cholesterol
40 mg; 1195 kJ (285 cal)

Note: You can reduce
the amount of fat used
in these recipes by
using an oil spray, or by
brushing the wok with
a very thin layer of oil.

*Hokkien noodle and beef stir-fry (top) with
sweet and sour chicken stir-fry*

33

Vegetable and potato cakes

*Ready to eat in
  30 minutes
Makes 10 patties*

200 g butternut
  pumpkin, peeled and
  cut into small pieces
500 g potatoes, peeled
  and cut into small
  pieces
50 g broccoli, broken
  into small pieces
1 1/2 cups (200 g) frozen
  diced vegetables
1/2 cup (60 g) grated
  Cheddar
1/2 cup (50 g) dry
  breadcrumbs
2 tablespoons oil

1. Steam the pumpkin
and potato for
5 minutes until tender.
2. Meanwhile, bring a
pan of water to the boil
and cook the broccoli
and frozen vegetables
for 2–3 minutes, or
until just cooked. Drain
and place in a bowl.
3. Mash the potato and
pumpkin until smooth.
Add to the vegetables
with the Cheddar and
stir to combine.
4. Place the
breadcrumbs on a
plate. Take a 1/3 cup
of the mixture and
coat all over with the
breadcrumbs, gently
shaping the mixture
into thick round patties
as you coat them.

Repeat with the
remaining mixture.
5. Place the oil in a
large frying pan over
moderate heat. Cook
the patties, in two
batches, over medium-
high heat until they are
golden brown on both
sides. Drain on paper
towels. Serve with a
mixed salad.

NUTRITION PER PATTY
*Protein 4.5 g; Fat 8 g;
Carbohydrate 10 g; Dietary
Fibre 2.5 g; Cholesterol
6 mg; 590 kJ (140 cal)*

Mini meat pies

*Ready to eat in
  30 minutes
Makes 6*

1 tablespoon oil
1 onion, chopped
2 cloves garlic, crushed
250 g lean beef mince
425 g can crushed
  tomatoes
220 g can baked beans
1 tablespoon tomato
  paste
3 sheets ready-rolled
  puff pastry, thawed
2/3 cup (85 g) grated
  Cheddar

1. Preheat the oven to
very hot 240°C (475°F/
Gas 9) and put a
baking tray on the top
shelf. Heat the oil in a
frying pan, add the

onion and garlic and
cook until soft. Add the
beef mince and brown,
breaking up any lumps
with the back of a fork.
2. Add the tomatoes,
baked beans and
tomato paste. Boil for
3–5 minutes, stirring,
until the mixture
thickens slightly.
3. Meanwhile, lightly
grease 6 x 1-cup
(250 ml) muffin holes.
4. Using a 14 cm sauce
as a guide, cut 6 circles
from the pastry sheets.
Cut a small 'V' starting
from the centre of each
circle to the edge, about
2 cm wide at the edge.
Overlap the cut out
section to fit the pastry
into each tin, and press
the join together firmly.
5. Spoon the mixture
into the pastry and
divide the Cheddar
between the pies. Place
on the baking tray in
the oven and bake on
the top shelf for
15–20 minutes, or until
golden and the pastry
is cooked.

NUTRITION PER SERVE
*Protein 20 g; Fat 30 g;
Carbohydrate 30 g; Dietary
Fibre 4 g; Cholesterol
65 mg; 2005 kJ (480 cal)*

Note: This is a great
meal to prepare ahead
and freeze.

*Vegetable and potato cakes (top) with
Mini meat pies*

American sandwich

Ready to eat in 20 minutes
Serves 4

1 tablespoon oil
4 eggs
12 thick slices bread
2 tablespoons mayonnaise
2 cups (90 g) shredded lettuce
125 g shredded ham
3 Roma tomatoes, sliced

1. Heat the oil in a frying pan. Add the eggs and fry for 2–3 minutes, or until the white is cooked and the yolk is still runny.
2. Meanwhile, toast the bread, then spread one side with mayonnaise. Place a slice of toast on four plates. Divide the lettuce among the toast.
3. Place another slice of toast on top. Arrange the ham, tomato and egg on top of this piece of toast. Top with the final piece of toast, mayonnaise-side-down. Serve the sandwich cut into triangles.

NUTRITION PER SERVE
Protein 20 g; Fat 15 g; Carbohydrate 45 g; Dietary Fibre 3.5 g; Cholesterol 200 mg; 1665 kJ (395 cal)

Note: The ham can be substituted with barbecued chicken. Whole-egg mayonnaise has more flavour and less sugar than other types. Home-made mayonnaise should not be given to young children because it contains raw eggs.

Sloppy Joes

Ready to eat in 25 minutes
Serves 4

1 tablespoon oil
1 onion, chopped
400 g beef mince
1 tablespoon plain flour
1 cup (250 ml) beef stock
1/2 cup (125 g) tomato sauce
2 teaspoons Worcestershire sauce
4 hamburger buns
tomato slices, to serve
shredded lettuce, to serve

1. Heat the oil in a frying pan and cook the onion for 3 minutes, or until soft. Add the mince and cook for 5 minutes, or until the beef has browned, breaking up any lumps with a fork.
2. Sprinkle the flour over the beef, and cook, stirring, for 1 minute. Slowly pour in the stock, stirring to combine. Add the tomato sauce and Worcestershire sauce and mix well. Bring to the boil, reduce the heat to low, and simmer for 10 minutes.
3. Cut the hamburger buns in half and toast. Lay both halves on four plates and ladle the beef mixture over. Serve with the tomato slices and shredded lettuce on the side.

NUTRITION PER SERVE
Protein 30 g; Fat 18 g; Carbohydrate 60 g; Dietary Fibre 4 g; Cholesterol 65 mg; 2210 kJ (530 cal)

American sandwich (top) with Sloppy Joes

Fish kebabs

*Ready to eat in
  25 minutes
Serves 4*

*8 bamboo skewers
1/2 cup (125 ml) lemon
  juice
1 tablespoon chopped
  fresh parsley
1 tablespoon chopped
  fresh coriander
1 clove garlic, crushed
300 g firm white
  fish fillet, cut into
  3 cm cubes
200 g salmon fillet, cut
  into 3 cm cubes*

Corn salsa
*270 g can corn kernels,
  drained
1 large avocado, diced
1 tomato, diced
1 small red onion,
  finely chopped*

1. Soak the skewers in
a shallow dish of water
while preparing the
basting sauce.
2. Combine the lemon
juice, parsley, coriander
and garlic in a bowl.
Divide in half and set
aside. Thread the fish
onto the skewers,
alternating the white
fish and the salmon.
You should have about
3 pieces of white fish
and 2 pieces of salmon
on each skewer.
3. Heat a lightly
greased large frying
pan until hot. Cook

the fish skewers for
3–5 minutes, or until
cooked through,
turning frequently. Use
half the lemon mixture
to brush over the
kebabs as they cook.
4. To make the corn
salsa, place all the
ingredients in a bowl.
Pour over the remaining
lemon mixture and toss
gently to combine.
5. Place 2 skewers on
each plate and serve
with the salsa and
some steamed rice.

NUTRITION PER SERVE
*Protein 30 g; Fat 10 g;
Carbohydrate 15 g; Dietary
Fibre 3.5 g; Cholesterol
75 mg; 1240 kJ (295 cal)*

Salmon cakes

*Ready to eat in
  30 minutes
Makes 10 cakes*

*600 g floury potatoes,
  peeled and cubed
415 g can salmon,
  bones removed,
  drained and mashed
1 small onion, finely
  chopped
1 egg, lightly beaten
1/2 cup (60 g) grated
  cheese
2 tablespoons chopped
  fresh parsley
1/2 cup (50 g) dry
  breadcrumbs
oil, for frying*

1. Place the potato
pieces in a large pan of
salted water and bring
to the boil. Cook for
about 5 minutes, or
until the potato is
tender. Drain well
and mash.
2. Place the mashed
potato in a large bowl,
add the mashed
salmon, onion, egg,
cheese and parsley. Stir
well to combine.
3. Place the
breadcrumbs on a
large plate. Spoon a
generous 1/3 cup of the
salmon mixture onto
the breadcrumbs.
Shape into a round
and coat well with the
breadcrumbs, then
flatten slightly. Repeat
with the remaining
mixture.
4. Heat 1 cm oil in a
large frying pan. Place
the salmon cakes in the
pan, in batches if
necessary, and cook
over medium heat for
2–3 minutes on each
side, or until golden
brown. Drain well on
paper towels and
serve immediately
with some mixed
salad leaves.

NUTRITION PER CAKE
*Protein 15 g; Fat 10 g;
Carbohydrate 10 g; Dietary
Fibre 1.5 g; Cholesterol
55 mg; 845 kJ (200 cal)*

*Fish kebabs (top) with
Salmon cakes*

Two-minute noodle and vegetable omelette

Ready to eat in 25 minutes
Serves 4–6

2 x 85 g packets chicken or tomato flavoured instant noodles
300 g frozen mixed vegetables
5 eggs, lightly beaten
1/3 cup (80 ml) milk
3/4 cup (90 g) grated Cheddar
2 tablespoons chopped fresh parsley
1 tablespoon oil

1. Bring a large pan of water to the boil and add the noodles with the flavour sachet. Stir to combine, then boil for 2 minutes, drain and set aside.
2. Bring another pan of water to the boil, add the frozen vegetables and cook for 1–2 minutes, or until heated through. Drain well.
3. In large bowl, combine the vegetables, noodles, eggs, milk, cheese and parsley and season with salt and pepper. Toss gently using two forks.
4. Preheat the grill.

Heat the oil in a 20 cm ovenproof non-stick frying pan. Pour the noodle mixture into the pan, using a fork to spread the noodles and vegetables out evenly.
5. Cook over medium heat for 3–5 minutes, or until the eggs have almost set. Place under a grill for 3–5 minutes, or until the top has set and is slightly golden. Cool slightly, then cut into wedges and serve with a salad.

NUTRITION PER SERVE (6)
Protein 10 g; Fat 20 g; Carbohydrate 5 g; Dietary Fibre 3 g; Cholesterol 165 mg; 835 kJ (200 cal)

Cheesy chicken macaroni

Ready to eat in 20 minutes
Serves 6

2 cups (310 g) macaroni
1/2 cup (80 g) frozen peas
1 1/2 cups (375 g) ricotta cheese
1/2 cup (50 g) grated Parmesan
2 tablespoons extra virgin olive oil
1/2 barbecue chicken, cut into bite-size pieces
1 large tomato, diced
1/3 cup (10 g) chopped fresh flat-leaf parsley
3/4 cup (90 g) shredded Cheddar

1. Bring a large pan of salted water to the boil and cook the macaroni according to the manufacturer's instructions, adding the frozen peas to the pan just before the macaroni finishes cooking. Drain well.
2. Meanwhile, put the ricotta cheese, Parmesan and oil in a pan. Mix to combine and place over a medium-low heat. Season with salt and black pepper. Add the chicken, tomato and parsley. Heat through until hot, then keep warm over a low heat. Preheat the grill.
3. Place the macaroni and peas in a shallow ovenproof dish about 20 x 30 cm. Add the chicken mixture and toss to combine. Sprinkle the Cheddar over the surface.
4. Place under the grill and cook until the cheese melts and browns. Serve with some vegetables.

NUTRITION PER SERVE
Protein 30 g; Fat 25 g; Carbohydrate 35 g; Dietary Fibre 3.5 g; Cholesterol 100 mg; 2065 kJ (495 cal)

Two-minute noodle and vegetable omelette (top) with Cheesy chicken macaroni

Fettucine with ham and corn

*Ready to eat in
  20 minutes*
Serves 4

400 g fettucine
2 x 310 g cans
  creamed corn
1 cup (125 ml) cream
80 g ham, cut into
  strips
2 tablespoons finely
  chopped fresh parsley

1. Fill a large pan with salted water and bring to the boil. Add the fettucine, stir well to separate the strands and cook according to the manufacturer's instructions. Drain well.
2. Meanwhile, heat the creamed corn and cream in another pan until boiling, then reduce the heat and add the ham. Simmer for 3 minutes and season to taste with salt and freshly ground black pepper.
3. Divide the fettucine among four serving plates and pour over the ham and corn sauce. Toss gently, then scatter with the parsley and serve.

NUTRITION PER SERVE
*Protein 15 g; Fat 15 g;
Carbohydrate 95 g; Dietary
Fibre 10 g; Cholesterol
40 mg; 2475 kJ (590 cal)*

Vegetable stir-fry

*Ready to eat in
  30 minutes*
Serves 4

2 tablespoons
  peanut oil
250 g firm tofu, cut
  into cubes
2 cloves garlic, crushed
1 teaspoon grated
  fresh ginger
1 zucchini, halved
  lengthways and sliced
1 carrot, halved
  lengthways and sliced
1 small red capsicum,
  cut into short
  thin strips
150 g small broccoli
  florets
2 tablespoons teriyaki
  marinade sauce
1/4 cup (60 ml) orange
  juice
1 tablespoon honey
1 tablespoon sesame
  seeds

1. Heat the wok until very hot, then add 1 tablespoon of the peanut oil and swirl to coat the sides. Fry the tofu in batches until golden, adding more oil if necessary. Remove from the pan and drain on paper towels.
2. Add the remaining oil to the wok and stir-fry the garlic and ginger for 1 minute.
Add the zucchini, carrot, capsicum and broccoli and stir-fry over a high heat for 3–4 minutes.
3. Return the tofu to the wok with the teriyaki marinade sauce, orange juice and honey. Toss to coat in the sauce and stir-fry for 2–3 minutes. Sprinkle with sesame seeds and serve with some steamed rice or noodles.

NUTRITION PER SERVE
*Protein 7 g; Fat 15 g;
Carbohydrate 10 g; Dietary
Fibre 3.5 g; Cholesterol
0 mg; 645 kJ (155 cal)*

*Fettucine with ham and corn (top) wit
Vegetable stir-fr*

PIZZAS

Beef and cherry tomato pizzas

Add oil to a frying pan and cook 2 steaks sliced into strips with 2 crushed cloves of garlic until browned. Spread 4 small pizza bases with a thin layer of tomato paste mixed with a teaspoon of mixed herbs. Sprinkle with grated cheese and top with half a red onion cut in wedges, the beef and a few halved cherry tomatoes. Bake for 10 minutes in a hot 220°C (425°F/ Gas 7) oven until the bases are golden and crisp. Sprinkle with shredded basil.

Mexican pizza

Fry a chopped onion and 2 crushed cloves of garlic in a little oil until soft. Add 400 g lean minced beef and fry, breaking up any lumps witrh a wooden spoon, until well browned. Add some taco seasoning and half a can of refried beans and stir to combine. Spread 2 large pizza bases with a little taco sauce, top with the mince and sprinkle with grated mozarella. Bake for 10–15 minutes in a hot 220°C (425°F/ Gas 7) oven, or until the bases are golden ·and crisp. Serve topped with guacamole and sour cream.

Stir-fry vegetable pizza

In a wok or large, heavy-based frying pan, stir-fry a packet of frozen chow-mein vegetable mix with 2 crushed cloves of garlic and a good splash of oyster sauce over high heat until th vegetables are just tender and cooked through and almost al the sauce has evaporated off. Spread a large pizza base with a thin layer of tomato paste and sprinkle ove a layer of grated mozarella. Top with th stir-fried vegetables an a sprinkling of sesame seeds.

ake for about
0 minutes in a hot
20°C (425°F/Gas 7)
ven, or until the base
golden and crisp.

Chicken tikka masala pizza

dd some oil to a
ying pan and cook
50 g chicken strips
ntil golden brown and
ooked through. Add
teaspoons of tikka
asala paste and cook
or 1 minute, or until
ne chicken is coated in
ne paste. Transfer to a
owl and stir in
tablespoons thick
ain yoghurt. Spread a
rge pizza base with

a layer of mango
chutney. Top with the
chicken strips and
bake in a hot 220°C
(425°F/Gas 7) oven for
10–15 minutes, or until
the base is golden and
crisp. Sprinkle over
some chopped fresh
coriander and drizzle
with extra yoghurt.

Ham and pineapple pizza

Spread 2 large
Lebanese breads evenly
with a thin layer of
tomato paste. Top the
tomato paste with a
handful of thin ham

strips and a few pieces
of chopped fresh or
well-drained canned
pineapple. Sprinkle
with a generous layer
of grated mozzarella
cheese and bake for
about 10 minutes in a
hot 220°C (425°F/
Gas 7) oven, or until
the bases are golden
and crisp.

From left to right:
Beef and cherry
tomato; Mexican;
Stir-fry vegetable;
Chicken tikka masala;
Ham and pineapple

45

Chicken burritos

*Ready to eat in 30
minutes
Makes 8*

375 g packet flour
  tortillas
  barbecued chicken
325 g jar mild salsa
2 large tomatoes,
  sliced
2 cups (135 g) shredded
  lettuce
  Lebanese cucumber,
  sliced
2 cups (250 g) grated
  Cheddar

1. Preheat the oven
to moderate 180°C
(350°F/Gas 4). Wrap
the flour tortillas
in foil and place on a
baking tray. Warm in
the oven for about
10 minutes.
2. Meanwhile skin,
bone and shred the
barbecued chicken.
Place the chicken in a
pan with the jar of
salsa and stir together
until heated through.
Arrange some of the
shredded chicken
and the sauce in the
middle of each of the
warm tortillas.
3. Pile the tomato,
lettuce, cucumber and
cheese on top of the
chicken in the tortillas.
Roll up and serve.

*Chicken burritos (top) with
Porcupine balls with pasta*

NUTRITION PER BURRITO
*Protein 10 g; Fat 15 g;
Carbohydrate 3.5 g; Dietary
Fibre 1.5 g; Cholesterol
30 mg; 806 kJ (185 cal)*

Porcupine balls
with pasta

*Ready to eat in 30
minutes.
Serves 4*

250 g beef mince
1/2 onion, chopped
2 cloves garlic, crushed
1/2 carrot, grated
1 teaspoon dried mixed
  herbs
1/2 cup (110 g)
  short-grain rice
150 g pasta wheels,
  twirls or any variety
  your kids like
500 g can tomato
  soup
1/2 cup (125 ml) milk
1 tablespoon chopped
  fresh parsley
3 tablespoons grated
  Parmesan, for serving

1. Combine the beef
mince, onion, garlic,
carrot, mixed herbs,
rice and some salt and
freshly ground black
pepper in a large bowl.
Mix well with your
hands and roll into
16 equal-sized balls.
2. Heat the tomato
soup, milk and
1 1/2 cups (375 ml)
water together in a pan.

Once the mixture
comes to the boil,
reduce the heat and
add the meatballs.
3. Cook the meatballs
for about 20 minutes,
stirring occasionally,
until the rice and meat
are cooked through.
When the meatballs
have finished cooking,
stir in the parsley.
4. Meanwhile, fill a
large pan with salted
water and bring to
the boil. Add the pasta
and cook according to
the manufacturer's
instructions. Drain well.
5. Divide the pasta
among four plates and
place the porcupine
balls and tomato sauce
on top. Serve with
the Parmesan.

NUTRITION PER SERVE
*Protein 25 g; Fat 10 g;
Carbohydrate 65 g; Dietary
Fibre 6 g; Cholesterol
50 mg; 1925 kJ (460 cal)*

Note: You can cook
this dish in the
microwave if you wish.
Place in a microwave-
proof dish and cook on
Medium-High for
10 minutes, or until
the rice and meat are
cooked through. The
meatballs can also be
made in advance and
frozen for up to
3 months if you wish.
Place in a plastic
container and seal well.
Defrost before using.

Lamb cutlets with apple, walnut and carrot salad

*Ready to eat in
20 minutes
Serves 4*

*500 g floury potatoes,
peeled and cubed
8 lamb cutlets,
well trimmed
1 tablespoon light
olive oil
2–3 tablespoons
mint jelly
3 tablespoons milk
40 g butter*

**Apple, walnut and
carrot salad**

*1¹/2 carrots, coarsely
grated
1 red apple, unpeeled
and coarsely grated
1 stick celery, finely
sliced
1/4 cup (30 g) walnut
pieces
2 teaspoons finely
chopped fresh mint
3 tablespoons coleslaw
dressing*

1. Place the potato in a large pan of salted water, bring to the boil and cook for 8 minutes, or until tender. Preheat the grill to medium hot.
2. Brush the lamb cutlets on both sides with the olive oil, then spread a thin coating of mint jelly over them. Place under the hot grill and cook for 2–3 minutes each side until browned and cooked through.
3. To make the apple, walnut and carrot salad, place the carrot, apple, celery, walnuts, mint and coleslaw dressing in a large bowl and mix together well.
4. Drain the potatoes, then mash with milk and butter. Season with salt and black pepper.
5. Spoon a pile of mashed potato onto each of four plates. Arrange two cutlets on top and serve with the salad.

NUTRITION PER SERVE
Protein 18 g; Fat 25 g; Carbohydrate 25 g; Dietary Fibre 4 g; Cholesterol 75 mg; 1710 kJ (410 cal)

Honey sesame meatballs

*Ready to eat in
30 minutes
Makes 24 meatballs*

*500 g lean beef mince
2 tablespoons soy sauce
1 egg, lightly beaten
1/4 cup (25 g) dry
breadcrumbs
1 tablespoon honey
1/2 cup (80 g) sesame
seeds
2 tablespoons oil*

1. In a bowl, combine the mince, soy, egg, breadcrumbs and honey. Using wet hands, roll tablespoonfuls of the mince mixture into balls and set aside on a plate.
2. Place the sesame seeds on a plate and roll the balls in them, pressing on firmly. Heat the oil in a large non-stick frying pan and cook the meatballs in batches over medium heat, turning carefully, until golden and cooked. Drain on paper towels and serve as snacks on cocktail sticks or with rice.

NUTRITION PER MEATBALL
Protein 5.5 g; Fat 6 g; Carbohydrate 2 g; Dietary Fibre 0.5 g; Cholesterol 20 mg; 340 kJ (80 cal)

Note: Don't give cocktail sticks to small children.

Lamb cutlets with apple, walnut and carrot salad (top) with Honey sesame meatballs

Herb and Parmesan-crusted fish with quick guacamole

*Ready to eat in
25 minutes
Serves 4*

1/4 cup (30 g) plain
flour, to coat
4 x 250 g skinless
fish fillets, cut into
2 pieces each (see
Note)
1 tablespoons dried
breadcrumbs
2 tablespoons grated
Parmesan
1 tablespoon chopped
fresh parsley
2 teaspoons chopped
fresh dill
1 tablespoon flaked
almonds, roughly
chopped
1 egg
1 tablespoon milk
2 tablespoons oil

Quick guacamole

200 g tub guacamole
dip
1 small ripe tomato,
deseeded and finely
chopped
1/2 onion, finely
chopped

1. Place the flour in a
shallow dish and coat
the fish evenly. Combine
the breadcrumbs,
Parmesan, parsley, dill

and almonds in a
shallow dish. Whisk
together the egg and
milk in another shallow
dish. Dip the fish into
the combined egg and
milk, then coat the fish
with the breadcrumb
mixture, ensuring the
crumbs are pressed
down firmly onto the
fish. Leave the fish to
stand while you make
the guacamole.
2. To make the
guacamole, combine
the dip, tomato and
onion in a small bowl.
3. Heat the oil in a
frying pan until hot.
Cook the fish over
medium heat for about
3 minutes each side, or
until golden brown and
cooked through.
4. Drain the fish on
paper towels and serve
with guacamole on top.
Accompany with salad
and oven-baked chips.

NUTRITION PER SERVE
*Protein 35 g; Fat 30 g;
Carbohydrate 10 g; Dietary
Fibre 2 g; Cholesterol
200 mg; 1900 kJ (455 cal)*

Note: Use a fish that
has few or no bones.
A good variety is fillet
of ling or blue-eyed
cod, which have only a
few easily removed
bones. Alternatively,
use fish cutlets.

Vegetable and macaroni soup

*Ready to eat in
30 minutes
Serves 4–6*

1 tablespoon oil
1 onion, cut into
1 cm cubes
1 large carrot, cut into
1 cm cubes
1 large zucchini, cut
into 1 cm cubes
1 litre chicken stock
1/2 cup (80 g) macaroni
1 tablespoon tomato
paste
300 g can kidney
beans, drained

1. Heat the oil in a
large pan, add the
vegetables and cook for
5 minutes, or until soft.
Meanwhile, bring the
stock to the boil. Add
the stock to the
vegetables and cover
with a lid to quickly
bring to the boil. When
boiling, uncover the
pan and cook for about
8 minutes, or until the
vegetables are tender.
2. Add the macaroni
and tomato paste.
Return to the boil and
cook for 8 minutes, or
until the pasta is tender.
Add the beans, salt and
pepper and stir until hot.

NUTRITION PER SERVE (6)
*Protein 5.5 g; Fat 3.5 g;
Carbohydrate 18 g; Dietary
Fibre 5 g; Cholesterol
0 mg; 545 kJ (130 cal)*

*Herb and Parmesan-crusted fish with quick
guacamole (top) and Vegetable and macaroni soup*

Sausage and pasta bake

Ready to eat in 30 minutes
Serves 6

2$\frac{1}{2}$ cups (225 g) penne pasta
10 thin sausages
1 small onion, chopped
2 carrots, diced
2 zucchini, diced
225 g can baked beans
425 g can crushed tomatoes
1 cup (125 g) grated Cheddar
$\frac{1}{2}$ cup (125 g) sour cream
2 tablespoons dry breadcrumbs

1. Bring a large pan of salted water to the boil and cook the pasta according to the manufacturer's instructions. Drain well.
2. Meanwhile, in a large frying pan, cook the sausages for 2–3 minutes, or until cooked through. Remove from the pan and slice into pieces.
3. Add the onion, carrot and zucchini to the pan. Cook over a medium-high heat for 2–3 minutes, or until the onion has softened. Add the baked beans and tomatoes, bring to the boil, then remove from the heat.

4. Preheat the grill. Mix together the vegetable mixture, sliced sausages, half the Cheddar, the sour cream and the cooked penne pasta. Spoon into a 2.5 litre ovenproof dish.
5. Sprinkle the remaining Cheddar and breadcrumbs over the top and grill until golden brown.

NUTRITION PER SERVE
Protein 15 g; Fat 25 g; Carbohydrate 40 g; Dietary Fibre 6 g; Cholesterol 55 mg; 1815 kJ (435 cal)

Pasta with chickpeas

Ready to eat in 30 minutes
Serves 6

3 cups (270 g) spiral pasta
1 tablespoon oil
1 large onion, chopped
2 cloves garlic, crushed
2 x 425 g cans crushed tomatoes
1 tablespoon tomato paste
425 g can chickpeas, drained
1 teaspoon dried Italian herbs
2 teaspoons sugar
1 cup (125 g) finely grated cheese

1. Bring a large pan of salted water to the boil and cook the pasta according to the manufacturer's instructions. Drain well.
2. Meanwhile, heat the oil in a large pan, add the onion and cook for 2–3 minutes, or until soft. Add the garlic and cook for 1 minute. Add the tomatoes, tomato paste, chickpeas, Italian herbs and sugar. Bring to the boil, reduce the heat and simmer for 10 minutes. Preheat the grill.
3. Return the pasta to the pan, then add the tomato mixture and stir to combine.
4. Transfer the mixture to a large shallow baking dish or six individual baking dishes, and sprinkle with the cheese. Cook under the grill until the cheese is just melted and bubbling. Serve with some steamed green vegetables.

NUTRITION PER SERVE
Protein 15 g; Fat 10 g; Carbohydrate 45 g; Dietary Fibre 7.5 g; Cholesterol 20 mg; 1495 kJ (355 cal)

Note: Borlotti or butter beans can be substituted for chickpeas if preferred.

Sausage and pasta bake (top) and Pasta with chickpeas

Sweet treats

Dessert is the best part of a meal for most kids. If you don't want to spend hours in the kitchen, try one of these quick ideas.

Little jellies

*Ready to eat in
  30 minutes*
Serves 6

2^{1}/$_{2}$ *cups (600 ml)
  freshly squeezed
  orange juice*
6 teaspoons gelatine
2 bananas
12 strawberries
yoghurt, to serve
*mint sprigs, to garnish,
  optional*

1. Pour ^{1}/$_{2}$ cup of the orange juice into a small heatproof bowl, sprinkle the gelatine in an even layer over the surface and leave to go spongy.
2. Place 1 cup of the orange juice in a small pan and bring to the boil. Turn off the heat and add the gelatine mixture, then stir until thoroughly dissolved.
3. Slice the bananas and strawberries and divide among six ^{1}/$_{2}$ cup (125 ml) ramekins or jelly dishes. Pour in the jelly (don't worry if the fruit floats). Put the jellies in the freezer for about 20 minutes, or until set.
4. Serve the jellies with a dollop of yoghurt and a mint sprig.

NUTRITION PER SERVE
*Protein 4 g; Fat 0 g;
Carbohydrate 20 g; Dietary
Fibre 1.5 g; Cholesterol
0 mg; 440 kJ (105 cal)*

Note: These jellies do not turn out of the moulds very well, so set them in glasses or jelly dishes. Do not leave in the freezer if you aren't serving them straight away. Move to the refrigerator as soon as they are set.

Little jellies

Rocky road

*Ready to eat in
30 minutes
Serves 8*

175 g milk chocolate,
chopped
40 g Copha (white
vegetable shortening),
chopped
100 g mini pink
and white
marshmallows
1/3 cup (30 g)
desiccated coconut
1/3 cup (70 g) glacé
cherries, halved
1/3 cup (45 g)
macadamia pieces

1. Lightly grease a
19 cm square cake tin.
Line the base and sides
with non-stick baking
paper, leaving a little
hanging over each side
so you can lift the rocky
road out of the tin.
2. Combine the
chocolate and Copha in
a heatproof bowl. Bring
a pan of water to the
boil, then remove the
pan from the heat. Sit
the bowl over the pan,
making sure the bottom
of the bowl is not
sitting in the water.
Stir the chocolate
occasionally until it has
melted. (Alternatively,
microwave on High for
1 minute, stirring twice

during cooking.)
3. Combine the
chocolate and the
remaining ingredients
in a bowl, spread over
the base of the
prepared tin and
smooth the surface.
Freeze the rocky road
for 15–20 minutes, or
until set. Cut into
pieces to serve.

NUTRITION PER SERVE
*Protein 4 g; Fat 25 g;
Carbohydrate 35 g; Dietary
Fibre 1 g; Cholesterol
8.5 mg; 1550 kJ (352 cal)*

Chocolate-coated bananas

*Ready to eat in
30 minutes
Serves 4*

2 bananas
4 paddle pop sticks or
a pair of disposable
chopsticks
1/3 cup (80 ml)
Chocolate Ice Magic
2 tablespoons sprinkles,
hundreds and
thousands or nuts

1. Peel the bananas and
cut each one in half
lengthways. Push the
paddle pop sticks
gently into the bananas
to make a handle.
(If you're using
chopsticks, break them
in half first.)

2. Warm the Chocolate
Ice Magic in a pan or
microwave according
to the manufacturer's
instructions, then pour
the chocolate into a tall
narrow glass. Twirl the
bananas in the
chocolate and place on
a baking tray lined with
baking paper. (You will
find that you have
excess chocolate, but
you need enough so
you can twirl the
bananas around in the
chocolate and coat
them evenly.)
3. If you want the
bananas to have a
thicker coat of
chocolate, allow them
to set in the freezer for
5 minutes, then recoat
them in the Chocolate
Ice Magic.
4. Tip the sprinkles
or hundreds and
thousands on to
separate plates for each
colour and roll the
bananas in them while
the coating is still wet.
5. Put the bananas on
a plate and place in the
freezer for 10 minutes
to set.

NUTRITION PER SERVE
*Protein 1 g; Fat 0 g;
Carbohydrate 25 g; Dietary
Fibre 1.5 g; Cholesterol
0 mg; 415 kJ (100 cal)*

Note: The bananas can
be made and left in the
freezer until needed if
you wish.

*Rocky road (top) with
Chocolate-coated bananas*

Fresh fruity slushies

*Ready to eat in
30 minutes
Makes 4*

250 g fresh
  strawberries,
  trimmed and
  washed
1 banana, sliced
1/3 cup (80 ml) milk
200 g tub flavoured
  yoghurt (any flavour
  you like)
plastic cups or ice-
  block moulds
  (available from
  some supermarkets)

1. Place the
strawberries, banana,
milk and yoghurt in a
food processor or
blender, and process
until slightly chunky or
smooth, depending on
the texture you prefer.
2. Pour the mixture
into the plastic cups or
ice-block moulds.
3. Place in the freezer
for about 25 minutes,
then stir the frozen
edges into the centre
of the slushies and
serve immediately.

NUTRITION PER SLUSHY
*Protein 5 g; Fat 3 g;
Carbohydrate 15 g; Dietary
Fibre 2 g; Cholesterol
8.5 mg; 435 kJ (105 cal)*

Note: If you want, you
can make these into
solid ice pops by
freezing them until
semi-frozen, then
pushing paddle pop
sticks into them.
Return to the freezer
and freeze until solid.
When you are ready
to eat them, remove the
frozen slushies from
freezer, then take them
out of the moulds.

Frûche and fruit salad

*Ready to eat in
10 minutes
Serves 4*

1/2 small pineapple,
  peeled, cored and
  cut into cubes or
  1 small can of
  pineapple pieces.
1 red apple, cored
  and chopped
  into cubes
1 banana, peeled
  and sliced
1 cup (180 g) red
  grapes, pips
  removed or 1 cup
  (200 g) stoneless
  cherries
2 x 200 g tubs vanilla
  or flavoured Frûche
  (fromage frais)

1. Toss all the fruit
together in large bowl,
then divide about half
the fruit evenly into
four 1 cup (250 ml)
capacity glass tumblers
or dishes.
2. Stir the Frûche gentl
to soften. Top with ha
the Frûche, then place
the remaining fruit on
top to make a third
layer. Finish with a
fourth layer of the
remaining Frûche.

NUTRITION PER SERVE
*Protein 2 g; Fat 4 g;
Carbohydrate 25 g; Dietar
Fibre 3 g; Cholesterol
0 mg; 885 kJ (200 cal)*

Note: Use any fruit in
season for this recipe.
Try oranges, pears and
stone fruits. You can
also use yoghurt
instead of Frûche if
you prefer.

*Fresh fruity slushies (top
with Frûche and fruit sala*

oached fruit ith waffles and oney yoghurt

*eady to eat in
15 minutes
rves 4*

*4 cup (90 g) honey
large green apples,
peeled, cored and
quartered
large firm ripe pears,
peeled, cored and
quartered
waffles
x 200 g tubs
honey-flavoured
yoghurt*

Place the honey and
cup (250 ml) water in
large pan and bring
the boil.
Cut the apple and
ear quarters in half
ngthways. Add the
uit to the honey
rup. Cover and
ook over a low heat
r 8 minutes, stirring
casionally, until the
uit is tender.
To serve, warm the
affles in the oven or
icrowave according
the manufacturer's
structions.
Place one or two
affles on each plate.
rrange some of the
ple and pear on the
affles, then pour over

the cooking syrup. Top
with a dollop of honey-
flavoured yoghurt and
serve immediately.

NUTRITION PER SERVE
*Protein 5 g; Fat 4.5 g;
Carbohydrate 45 g; Dietary
Fibre 2.5 g; Cholesterol
15 mg; 1324 kJ (300 cal)*

Fruity barbecue kebabs

*Ready to eat in
20 minutes
Makes 8 kebabs*

*8 bamboo skewers
(see Note)
1 kiwi fruit
1/2 small pineapple
2 bananas
1 green apple
8 strawberries
1/4 cup (90 g) honey
1/4 cup (60 ml) orange
juice*

1. Soak the bamboo
skewers in water while
you prepare the fruit.
2. Peel and cut the kiwi
fruit into eight even-
sized pieces. Remove
the skin and core from
the pineapple, and cut
into 3 cm pieces. Cut
the bananas into
8 even-sized pieces. Peel
and core the apple and
cut into eight even-
sized pieces. Remove
the hulls from the
strawberries.

3. Thread one piece
of each fruit onto the
bamboo skewers in a
pretty pattern.
4. Preheat a barbecue
hot plate or an oven
grill. Combine the
honey and orange juice
in a small bowl.
5. Brush the honey
and juice over the fruit
and cook for about
6 minutes, turning
halfway through
cooking. Take care not
to overcook or the fruit
will fall off the skewers.
Brush with the honey
and juice mixture
during the cooking.
6. Serve the fruit
skewers with a little of
the honey and juice
mixture drizzled over.
Delicious with yoghurt
or ice cream.

NUTRITION PER KEBAB
*Protein 1.5 g; Fat 0 g;
Carbohydrate 25 g; Dietary
Fibre 2.5 g; Cholesterol
0 mg; 465 kJ (110 cal)*

Note: It is important to
soak the skewers first
or they will burn on the
barbecue. You can use
short or long skewers
for this recipe.
You can also use any
fruit on the skewers,
provided it is not too
soft, or it may fall off
as it cooks. Remove the
fruit from the skewers
if you are serving these
fruity kebabs to very
young children.

*oached fruit with waffles and honey yoghurt
op) with Fruity barbecue kebabs*

DRINKS

Strawberry soy thickshake

For each person, place half a glass of vanilla-flavoured soy milk, a scoop of vanilla or strawberry tofu ice cream, a handful of strawberries and a tablespoon of honey in a blender. Blend until smooth and thick, then pour into tall glasses to serve.

Fruit crush

For each person, place about 6 ice cubes in a plastic bag and crush them with a meat mallet or rolling pin. Place the crushed ice in a blender with 1/4 glass of pineapple juice and 1/2 glass of fresh orange and mango juice. Blend until combined, then pour into tall glasses to serve.

Iced banana smoothie

For each person, put a banana, 3/4 glass of milk, a scoop of vanilla ice cream, and 2 teaspoons of honey in a blender. Blend until smooth, then pour into glasses and dust with a little ground cinnamon

❖ FAST KIDS' FOOD ❖

Cola ice cream soda

or each person, fill
tall glass up to
alfway full with cola,
nen add a scoop of
anilla ice cream. The
e cream will make the
la foam up, so serve
mediately. For a
ariation, you could
try lemonade instead
of cola.

Fruity punch

Combine 10 chopped
strawberries, 1/2 peeled
and chopped pineapple,
2 peeled and segmented
oranges and 2 peeled
and chopped kiwi fruit
in a large punch bowl
(you can change the
fruit depending on the
season). Add 2 glasses
of pineapple juice,
2 glasses of dry ginger
ale and 2 glasses of
lemonade and stir
gently to combine. Stir
in 2 tablespoons
chopped fresh mint
leaves and ladle
into 6–8 glasses
to serve.

Warm chocolate marshmallow drink

For each person, put
a mug full of milk in a
pan. Add 1 tablespoon
drinking chocolate per
mug and stir over a low
heat until dissolved.
When dissolved, turn
up the heat until the
chocolate is hot, then
pour back into the
mug. Top each with a
spoonful of whipped
cream, marshmallows
and drinking chocolate.

*From left to right:
Strawberry soy
thickshake; Fruit
crush; Iced banana
smoothie; Cola ice cream
soda; Fruity punch;
Warm chocolate
marshmallow
drink*

63

Index